The Yellow Transparents

The Yellow Transparents

JOAN ALESHIRE

FOUR WAY BOOKS

Marshfield

Editorial Office
Four Way Books
PO Box 607
Marshfield, MA 02050

Library of Congress Catalog Card Number: 96-86553

ISBN 1-884800-13-0

Cover design by Zuzzolo Graphics, Inc.
Text design by Acme Art, Inc.
Manufactured in the United States of America
This book is printed on acid-free paper.
Four Way Books is a division of Friends of Writers, Inc.,
a Vermont-based not-for-profit organization.

ACKNOWLEDGMENTS

The following poems have appeared in the following periodicals,
sometimes in different form: *Caprice*: "Days As Gray and Brown";
Crazyhorse: "Addiction"; "Trips to the Cleaner's"; *Cream City Review*:
"Body of Earth"; "World's End"; *Crab Orchard Review*: "Dog Star";
"Imaginary Twin"; *Green Mountains Review:* "The Fern in the Well,
Fruitlands"; "Women in the Water"; *Indiana Review*: "Cheek to Cheek";
Jacaranda Review: "Door to Door"; *Marlboro Review*: "Ferry Permit";
The Nation: "Air Show"; "Full Flower Moon"; *Poetry*: "Top of the
World"; "Healing"; *Seneca Review*: "Wake"; "Break of Day: After Col-
ette"; "The Yellow Transparents"; *Warren Wilson Review*: "Milkhouse";
"Rural Delivery." "Full Flower Moon" was reprinted here. And in the
following anthologies: *Decade (New Letters)*: "Color"; "Cheek To
Cheek"; "Full Flower Moon" (reprinted); *Quarterly Review of Literature
40th Anniversary Anthology* 1994: "The Children"; "Full Flower Moon"
(reprinted); "Into History"; "Use"; *Staring Back, Disabled Writers on
Disability* ed. Kenny Fries. Dutton (forthcoming in 1996): "Expecta-
tion"; "The X-Rays"

Thanks to the editors of these publications, and to Martha Rhodes,
Ellen Bryant Voigt, and Renate Wood for their suggestions on this
manuscript. The community of writers in the MFA Program at Warren
Wilson College continues to be an inspiration, stimulation and support.
Sid Atkins and Calen Erb helped with their computer skills and their
good-natured patience, as the poems went through draft after draft.

This book is published in loving memory of Mitch Spencer.

CONTENTS

I.

II.

III.

I

THE FERN IN THE WELL: FRUITLANDS

Where the farm failed,
we stepped as they stepped,
on flagstones the ground hadn't yet
pulled under; touched the hand-forged heart
latching the door. The prim, fresh-painted house
gave no hint of what went on: palmprints
staining the stairwell wall, crumbs
dusting the floor, oat-caked plates,
hammocks of cobweb, weeds dominant
in the dooryard. Abba and her girls
hauling flax before the storm,
while Bronson floated to meetings,
talking *emancipation, celibacy,*
community, animal-respecting farms.
Abba weak from carrying the weight,
the new baby, Louisa May at ten — afraid —
hauled the wash, the oats, baled hay,
braided flax into shoes,
swept, scrubbed, hoed the hard ground
anyone but Bronson could see
is dense with ledge and perilously steep.

The water in the well was too far down
to reflect us — two friends and a child
leaning to catch its glint, amazed
at the curl of fern growing from such slight
cracks between the stones, green
though the grass around us was winter-brown.
Was it a hard passage — the plant
pushing its leaf around stone?
Or did it sense the opening, knowing this
the only place to unfurl?

The stones press their cold weight down,
but the thin stem curves up
in its green urge, and fans out,

as a life like Louisa's — circumscribed,
beset — finds a narrow channel
and takes form. Wouldn't she call it
nothing heroic? It's unstoppable,
this being born.

THE X-RAYS

They looked like photographs of trees,
except that the terms were reversed —
black for the background, white
for the object itself. And light
shone though the white, making it
insubstantial, subject to change —
but that was my vision, my hope.

There was a smell of hot metal, the charge
of early inventions, and I had to lay
each arm flat on a glossy black plate
that reflected the past and future
with their endless questions. Not to
move, not even to breathe, to act only
as object, so the kindly men, friends
of my father, could hold the film
against the light, admiring the clarity,
admitting the mystery.

No one said *tree* to me, but I saw
the photographs of dancers and the apple trees
they mimicked in "Appalachian Spring,"
curved and twisting; and the cypresses
pressed by wind that Weston took at Point Reyes.

Deformed was the description, and I agreed
since it was simplest to, though that means
unnatural. Trees respond, in thick joint,
the gnarl, the odd turn, to some force, some
weather. What after all is form
but the giving in, the inch-by-inch bend,
and then the resistance?

CEDAR-POST FENCE

Gardens have attached even the rough,
uncultivated places — those half-
and quarter-acres overlooked by lawns.
Ivy escaped a border once; it's annexed the trees.
Some green strands twine the fence
that separates back road from the house
where so much of our time went.
Cedar posts shaggy with bark,
six foot spears with no grips or toeholds,
made to keep someone like me —
outsider, suspect now —
from seeing in, trying to remember.

Brown velvet curtains made theaters
we were forbidden to play in;
our playhouse half-hid in ferns
that gave when we brushed them
an ancient scent. The lion's head
embedded in the sunporch pool's
blue tile opened a mouth we believed
full of water. Your uncle the pilot,
back from prison camp a hero,
confirmed our belief in miracles.
The silver beech like a god's statue
gazed into its own reflecting pool.
We buried dead frogs around its edges,
and three days later looked to dig them up,
to see if the bodies had risen.

It was hard for us to find those graves
again; unmarked, shallow, we forgot
where they had been. Tunnels, piles of dirt —
moles had been there before us.
What we wanted was some proof
of transformation, though we believed
without it, in that world of imagining.

Then you were gone; no one and nothing
could change you back. I can locate
only the neighborhood where I had
and lost you, only narrow glimpses
in the fence that holds me back now.
What rushes through — the happiness,
the hurt intractable, which is to say real.

EXPECTATION

The Christmas Eve it snowed, hooves
rang sharp on the roof above my bed,
and small bells stamped the air
that came in a clean white slice
through my part-open window.
In the morning, I moved downstairs
on a crest of expectation; colored light
flooded past the half-closed door
as if the living-room held too much surprise.
The balsam with its reflecting globes
and unearthly birds had changed the place
to wildness. This world was mine:
the toy monkey set to move as I made him,
colored papers waiting for my hands.

How long did I believe a day would open
magically on every wish marked with my name?
I used to think I would wake entirely
changed: what was never there —
the missing fingers — there,
and beautifully straight besides:
hands like my friend's, intelligent and strong.
Even Christmas morning I found my distinguishing parts
in their crookedness entirely the same,
as they pulled the ribbons, tore the bright papers,
ran the metal motorcycle up the sofa's ridge
and down its slopes, pulled the monkey
on its red leash. The clay figures bending
to the nub of a baby I arranged and re-arranged:
the Wise Men coming from farther and farther off,
over steeper hills of sheet, holding their gifts.

Thinking you would come for me,
all those days with no sign — that
was the old hope of transformation.
I see us more clearly now. Expecting

nothing brings its own gifts — February light
coming back always a surprise:
so gold and open-handed.

BOTTOMLESS POND

Because we were forbidden
to go there, of course the pond
was where we went, when no one
seemed to be looking. A dog had drowned
there our mothers said — pulled under,
a black or Chesapeake brown retriever —
by the turtle that lived in the depth
of leaves that layered the bottom.
Or was it a swan that pulled the dog
to its death? White wings raised
in my dreams above the doomed black muzzle.
A retriever like mine, its strong chest
no defense against the clamp of the turtle beak,
swan beak dragging it underwater.

And so there was an awful
fascination — If we took the path
through the woods, beyond gardens,
out of sight of the house, we could
be there in instants.

I'm sure I persuaded her;
it's what I did, daring her. At first,
we only poked the pond's edges, eyeing
the layer of leaves below the surface
that made the pond seem shallow. With longer sticks
we tried to reach some center, half-hoping,
half-afraid something would take the bait.

No turtles, no fierce swan or pond-god
came at our prodding, and we trailed back
up the path, deflated. We hadn't even tried
to slip in the water.

That her mother had seen us
shocked us; she had been everywhere, like God.
She sent me outside, to hear the slap
of flesh to flesh, sobbing, silence.

Her face sore, red and swollen
as if stung by bees in the blossoms,
my friend climbed the plum tree
to escape me, refusing apology and consolation.
For all the games where I was the hero —
cape of Superman, cape of Prince Valiant —
I wouldn't throw myself in front of her
and take her mother's anger instead.

Carp suspend themselves now in the wintry water — orange slivers
like the last gum-tree leaves, above
the real leaves that keep the bottom
hidden. Albino fish, silverish submarines,
have given up exploring the depth
beneath them, where turtle and swan
feed on the dogs, on each other, on the mud,
on the answers that are lost to me, and the questions.

USE

How could they not have told me
I would be held down
and made to lose consciousness,
meaning myself?

Five,
I thought the men and women
with starched white coats, with puffs
on their heads like frozen breath,
with vials for blood, and needles,
with stretchers with straps,
with anaesthetizing enemas —
strangers who took me
from my mother, though
she let me go — acted as if they
had every right to my body.
I thought — it doesn't now
seem wrong — they were intent
on killing whatever was myself.

At what point did the ordinary trip to town
become a trap? Someone larger,
in white, moving toward me, closing
in. Only taking your
tonsils, they said; I was a dull,
trusting thing, and then
I began screaming so loud,
unbearably, energetically, relentless,
they let my mother come, though
I no longer believed her; she had
given in. They were rattled
by the sweat and flush
I had worked myself into,
the fever that would keep someone
of them awake all night to my delirium,
my small revenge.

Would reason
have persuaded me? They might have
led me easily then to the great Christ
stretching his marble arms — COME
UNTO ME — to all the sufferers: the sick,
the poor, the sellers of something
who made the hospital hall
part bazaar, part hell.

Older,
would I have believed it all
for good? The stern technician determined
to keep piercing my finger until she had
all she wanted of my blood. The furious
resident forcing the enema in?
I know I trouble them, and must
trouble them, though I am overwhelmed.
But what is this pleasure at the touch
that takes what it will? This longing
I will have and resist having,
to be taken up as a cat cradles the mouse
in its claws, holds it in a mouth
humming with desire.

CRACK IN THE WORLD

I didn't go back to look,
though rocks don't change
much in a life's space.
It would have seemed small,
the crack in the rock ledge
I thought went all the way
down. *Digging for China?*
they'd say when I played in the sand,
but this was much deeper, more serious:
jagged, narrow, at least three times
my height long. As far as I could see,
it went incalculably in.

It was my life's greatest project
then, filling the crack in the world
with chips of glass the sea had churned
smooth — frozen foam, stilled sun,
stretch of the ocean's hardest blue —
and only interesting stones:
freckled or lucky ones, banded by other stone
in amazing amalgamations. I took
whatever was free to be seized.
The crack would keep
snail turbans that fit my fingertip,
pearly ears where mussels lived,
bleached-green shields sea urchins used,
sand dollars someone had been spending.

Those afternoons easily come back,
pure in their concentration. The gathering
then was all. I had no sense
my body might lack something,
my birth cracked an ordered world.
Decisive as God, I spotted, seized,

filled the crevice with glass-shine,
stone-gloss, strange shapes that pleased me.
Nothing would be taken away. In my world
would be no emptiness.

LIFE-SIZED DOLL

The doll my own size
given for my fifth Christmas,
five days later was taken away.
I searched the rooms in disbelief:
nothing where the doll had been.

What had I done? What I couldn't
do, or help not doing. What notion
of purging the body of sin, excess,
had I transgressed?

Give us
the satisfaction, my mother meant
if not said, as if what my body made
was theirs not mine,
and a child could control it
by her will alone. There was a rule
for each of my moments, no privacy
in the white-rimmed room.

The doll would be gone, I understood,
until I ended my resistance. Good people
who gave me much, allowed much
I love, what could they
have been thinking? Some order in a book,
some passion for order, chiding a child
in the bewildered morning, uneventful noon,
anxious night, making the black-and-white tiles
of the bathroom floor part chessboard, part battleground.

Cod liver oil and mineral, cylinders of wax,
the water cure — I forgot what rid my body
five days later of its stubborn waste,
the part I came to love since it was so
demanded. Again my life meshed its cogs
with the rest; harmony ruled the house,

where I had the doll I'd longed for,
which now had no interest for me:
her face stiff and plaster-white, hair frozen
in its square, smooth cut, eyes wide and staring
straight ahead — of a certain blue depth,
made, I could tell, of glass that had been shattered
and reassembled: that part of her most like life.

NORTHEAST POOL

(MAINE, 1948)

Sailing that Sound, you can see from the ocean
how thin the wall of that world is — rickety slats
that take in a chunk of shore to civilize, damming
and warming the cold salt water. I remember mostly
what was underfoot, what I sensed along my skin,
cool and almost bare. Canvas-covered boardwalks shook
with our weight; we ran on slants and stairs
past the blaze of zinnia and nasturtium
where the most expensive bathhouses were,
with their uneven roofs, unsteady chairs — the signs
of old privilege: careless of its looks.

The wood deck was splinters beyond canvas;
we jumped to the graygreen gravel shifting
at the pool's salt edge. We stood ankle-
then knee-deep, maybe testing ourselves,
maybe forbidden to go on. I think we could
swim, my cousin and I, or were about to — buoyed
by salt but not going far. I thought it was
an open space; I didn't see the children begin
to ring us: a fire to get through.

I wanted to give them a password, an answer —
to own the mystery of myself — but I knew
no reason for what had happened, to make me
look different from them. Why some are chosen
to make distinctions visible — shade of pigment,
offense to symmetry, curve against grain,
missing piece. There was no friend here
to confirm I was *fine, a friend*. Bare in my swimsuit,
only knee-deep, I found no refuge in the water.

My cousin, younger and shy, could see it
all — me, the children pressing in, curious,
suspicious, as I threw definitions

to keep them at bay — *born this way,*
I can do everything. We were sent out
together; my cousin didn't choose.
She'd been behind, then I sensed her
beside me. We faced the other children — seconds
seeming our lifetimes — until they backed away.
Did an adult approach? I like to think
it was our stubbornness, making its own
ring of privilege: closing them out, keeping us safe inside.

COLOR

I'd go into her room without knocking,
presuming to sit on the bumpy chenille
on the over-varnished bed — somebody's cast-off,
backroom, make-do. I'd look at her magazines'
brown faces, wondering why the four men with girls'
voices *want a paper doll* — like mine? —
to call their own. Are they very
poor, I'd ask, and why do your dresses
have holes? Why are your hands pink
underneath when your skin is brown?
Because, she'd say, even, almost amused
that a child wouldn't know everything
hasn't a reason, a child wouldn't know
what colors mean. Because work has to be done
whether you want to or not, she took in
the storms I made, and in her broad silence
I was left calm. Trouble was her old man,
she'd say, get him laughing, hold out
her little finger, and wrap him around.

The man in the picture from those times —
"Harlem Apartment" — lies on a spread
of that same nubbed stuff, so stiff
my back twinges from watching him hold still
with sharp-pressed clothes, shiny shoes,
oiled-flat hair. He shuts his eyes hard
against the flash that pins him in permanence
against his wall papered with all the white
beauties in fashion then — Betty, Bette, and Rita —
who smile down on his poor attempt at sleep.
With all the best intentions, the pale man
behind the camera directs even his dreams.

Forty years gone, and the stranger who stops me
at the edge of the park breezes easy,
full of his life — "Smell the air!" —
humid as breath, sharp in pine and acacia.
"Don't waste it! Live!" He plays the edge,
pulling in whatever minnows will reel
at his shiny lures. He knows what will
entrance a slow fish — a bag of so much
white powder I think it's soap, a twist
of musty green his grandmother loved
for her blues. His cadence alone
is what I fall into, knowing where the beats
lie, sure, taking their time. Such skin as his
will be warm, accepting. Such hair like cloud,
and I want against reason to disappear in its depth.

BALLAST

Blue willow bent over a bridge, blue
pergola beside it, deep blue brook
become the fence that holds the rest —
each piece has the same ingredients,
though they stipple and swirl,
blue intensities of cobalt and sweat.

My mother's china wasn't stowed for itself
on the clippers sailing from China;
crates of it balanced the load —
rough, hand-thrown vessels that seemed
of no value. Souvenirs of the catch,
prized: a family's badge
of being first — bowls, plates, pots
stacked as tight in the holds
as human cargo was, and bound
for the rich country's pleasure.

Mary, at work for my mother,
lifts a stack of five from its shelf —
someone counted wrong this holiday,
my cousins line up for plates
Mary's to hand me. The stack wavers
between us, each piece unevenly thrown,
unconforming to the one below. It's an art
anyway, handling plates — one extending,
one accepting, balancing exactly give and take. So Mary lifts
five dinner plates down and holds them
out, as I notice her fingers more
than what they grasp: her skin deep
red-brown, with working wrinkles; the long,
fine ovals of her nails; the ring
with a flower woven into it,
not on the wedding digit.

She lets the china go,
into the mitt my hands make,
trusting I'm steady. Wasn't I
older, bending her to my will,
days her mother came to work
for mine and had no place to leave her?
In the album we're five or six,
but I'm twice her size; no one
should have a smile smug as mine,
such a plump white face. Mary's hair
shines, oiled and skinned from the knot
of her face: her frowning stare
at whoever thought to pose us together.
She seems to see the white luck
that will take me out of there, anywhere
I wanted, and leave her — just as I'd
choose the game and make her my second,
my valet, my — I have to say — slave.

The plates shudder in their passage
from her hands to mine: her giving, my taking.
Isn't our history here? I'm not sure
I have the shifting load, laugh in relief
I've balanced it in my hands. Mary gives back
no false assurance, false friendliness, poor
joke to make the rough smooth, or the china
ballast for an even sail. It's unavoidable,
the weight I list under, being the one
who thought I would change things.

DOOR TO DOOR

When the wind shifted to blue,
stirring the heat off the streets with salt
from the docks, we thought of beginnings,
though the sycamores shook
in their protective collars, and their leaves
crumbled, still green. We kept watering and feeding
the circles of earth in the asphalt, telling the children
to pat the scabbed trunks, not to make them
the ends of jump-rope turns, not chain
bicycles to them. I never knew which evening
might be the last, as he tried not to love
some other, said he was trying, until I wanted
to let it all go the way it was tending.
When the forces of order raised
their pale fists, I went door to door
to have some reason, though there were often
no doors to the urine-stained buildings.

Volunteers for the candidate who promised peace
went tandem, two to each walk-up eaten
from inside, two to the officially planned bland
cinderblock projects decorated with all their bold
I AM'S. In those days, you were killed, usually,
with some reason, some warning, and we went with our hopes
into each building, with our voting lists and promises
of change. People opened to us across the chains
of their caution, sometimes ushering us further,
to sit under portraits of Jesus, the Kennedys,
and Martin Luther King — oddly tinted as if
by morticians — those heroes who kept leaving us
to hope their images were worthy of our faith.
Surrounded by such longing, we'd offer miracles
of our own — the vote that would change the streets
to lawns, shotgun flats to whole houses, neighbors
living hard against one another to friends.
And the rats, with nothing to gnaw on, gone.

But even I who lived on hope began
to hear the lie. And when he caught and cried
against me, swearing he tried, I cried because
it seemed polite to, and went on to more doors.
The morning after the loss, power settled itself
in its usual seat, scratching its old balls
with no shame. The streets were dirtier even
than before, with all the handbills torn
and blowing, winter clamping on, no saviors
other than ourselves rising from anywhere.

BURDEN BASKET

Not always what we want, ancestors
stubborn in their pinched collars:
cool Indian fighter staring insistent
under the smart brim of his dandy's hat,
his wife keeping with an elegant slant
her diary where *Litle Lucy is born*
without pain or joy, *Weather continues*
hot, There are warnings of cyclones,
The cavalry brings many prisoners in.
No hint of the fear that made her
hate Indians: women who crowded her porch
until she bought enough of their baskets.

Women forced to wear uniform black dresses
wove what came to hand in the harsh new place —
oat, saxifrage, wheat, willow, keeping color
in the warp: black-brown bracken fern root,
blue-black devil's claw, red-bud trace.
They fought among themselves, so
Great-grandmother instructed the children
who would be my mother and aunts.
She kept of course none of the baskets;
no shallow scoops for winnowing wheat,
deep urns for beans, jugs to hold water.
No Burden Basket larger than the rest,
woven of rough willow-bark and smooth,
furred lengths of cloth and buckskin
hanging free, to stream behind
when the load was balanced on head, mid-back,
shoulders, and the bearer's step almost light.

Great-grandmother would have thought it
especially ugly, ungainly, let the children
fool with it — Lucy, who would seek
the strange and love the injured thing,
would have imagined the buckskin back,

those strips its mane and tail. Pinched
by high collars, buttoned shoes, asthma,
my grandmother will tell her children
I saw them bring Apache prisoners in:
braves manacled but sitting their ponies
as if inseparable from them, not noticing
her, Army's child, trapped in her little
white girl's body. Couldn't they see,
she wondered, how she was like them?
Seeing them bring the prisoners — her father
first with the flag on his pommel, red bands
like lash-marks under a glittering sky,
first with his stubborn eyes, his merciless spurs.

WOMEN IN THE WATER

My friend and her lover, two women,
cross the rock shore holding hands —
for balance, for love, unashamed
so to need each other, though the girl
we pass oiling her boyfriend's back
stares, not sure she's seen right,
across the few feet, the miles
between the usual and what's not.

Because I follow their slipping, steadying,
I can see how quickly the boyfriend rises
on his elbow to get a load of this
blissful innocence, willed ignorance
of him. If I knew more, I'd realize
it's safe here at the lake's edge:
stares don't follow as trucks do,
shifting down slow and insolent,
noticing lovers who look too much alike
in small towns at night, heaving out
a wad of spit or bottle that explodes
with surprising glitter into shards.

My friend can imitate the townspeople
falling back — *falling back* — with alarm
when she and Lynn, six kids between them,
took their covered dishes
to the church potluck. *We were parting
the Red Sea, we were walking on water ...*
She was the first I knew to let her hair fly free,
her feet go bare on Cambridge streets.
Her lover was the softest-voiced, most dangerous-
looking of the men, with his Harley,
engineer's boots, black leather. Ignited
together, no one could think them innocents.

The water takes us now — two together,
one alone — in its transparent power,
lifting the fine long hairs on two pairs of legs,
filling their loose suits, lulling bodies
already at ease. My hair fans in its length,
vain as I am of it and the smooth tusks
of my legs, as I move to be alone
with the water. The lovers, though, orbit
only each other: dipping, chaffing, treading
the lake's gentle pressure,
one never losing sight of her partner.
My friend basks, she lets herself
be wrapped: *Are you cold, are you cold?*
It's like being a child again, and
being a mother, they are so mutually tender,
covering themselves in the towel barely big enough for one,
disappearing into one room to peel their suits
and dress together, as I haven't with a woman
since age made us rivals and ashamed.

Alone in the other room, I strip
the resisting second skin, cover the cool flesh
that still tunes itself to the look of men
I love for their reckless lengths,
the long negotiations of distance
and desire. I have hurt women
who loved me more than I could love
back, wanting nothing so close
as these two are — or is it
too hard to follow my friend? She moves
into the stares, through the wall
of them, parts the Red Sea with her body.

A STILLNESS, ALMOST DROWNED

Other children too had stepped that way
in all ignorance — none of us was warned
of the steep drop from the shallow end
where even the smallest could easily sit —
to a place where all the self was lost:
gone under water. I remember how light
it was, how still without breathing,
and the strange way time slowed, and I
made no move to move. Suspended
by the water's silent way of having
its way, I lost all memory of kicking, pushing,
resisting — all the swimming I knew.

It must have been an enchantment, a taste
for perfect stillness my godmother pulled me
back from, abandoning sunglasses and cigarette —
true guardian, standing in for my mother and God —
her quick, tennis-toned arms clasped
under mine until my head broke
the placid surface that had covered me,

and I burned for air. I could have drowned
so easily then, or when the man I loved
a long time unnoticed finally reached for me.
There should have been some salt of sweat
or bitterness of beer in our mouths,
but all taste, all smell, even feeling
was gone, our bodies strangely dissolved,
as if desire disappears, its object met.
No sound reached us
from the crowd, or reached me.
Did the shock of kissing stun us equally
or was I the only one
sent out of myself, enthralled?

I know only that I stopped to breathe,
broken into my separateness, coming up
from the stillness of almost being drowned.
His eyes darkened; I could take no bearing
in that unrelieved, unreflecting depth.
He has been angry a long time, thinking me
insulting, even perverse. I couldn't help
what I saw: both of us suspended
under water, swayed by that airless
enchantment, in danger of staying down.

INTO HISTORY (1968)
— FOR MY DAUGHTER

A child then, you knew less
than we — but not by much —
what the cloud was, filling our ground-floor rooms,
stinging our eyes, burning our skin.
You understood less why that neighbor
let loose such an expression of his rage
into our yard, and those of the other
hippie niggerlovers on our block.
When the police came, after months
of observing, he cowered in a bedroom
filled with guns and swastika stars.

One end of the street dead, the other
exposed to Smith's hurtle of traffic,
fruit and fish markets in Spanish and
English, cut-rate furniture emporia,
botanicas and bodegas, gypsies
in storefronts — the short block
would vibrate, whatever wind blew
through the city, the country in those years.

The night after the murder in Memphis,
we heard it in the pavement, feet
pounding up from Smith, pausing, thudding
on, not in the patterns of tag
and stickball the kids carried out
in daylight, but a pace now bold,
now furtive under the vapor-light moons.

A whistle at a distance, a footfall
up close — through the slats
of the front-room blinds I saw
a human shape add itself to the shadow
of our van out front. A man or boy

set down the TV he must have carried
with difficulty, even on adrenaline,
out of a smashed window on Smith Street,
balanced beside it, crouched like a runner
waiting for the gun to start.

I called your father to watch with me;
you were asleep in the room I thought
serene: high-ceilinged, facing the backyard.
I thought it a cloister, though really
you had no distance from the workings
of that house. One then — your father and I
stared as the street was caught at both ends
by pincers of blue light, slamming doors,
shouts. In the middle the boy — did I mention
his dark skin? — tried to surrender or make
a reflexive run. At least six white cops
raised their fists, their nightsticks
over their heads, over his, and brought them down.

Your father ran outside cursing; I was close
behind, with Mrs. Mas from next door.
Mrs. Kelly up the block was yelling —
all the accents on the same words to stop
hitting the boy who had rolled himself small
and still they got in enough strikes
to his close shaved head that his groans
came from us. Mrs. Mas was crying to God
in Spanish then, but your father began
a boxer's dance, taunting the cops, until two
turned from their business and threatened
to take him too. Loud, foul-mouthed —
always someone in authority would see
the danger in him, something unbound.

That night he thrilled us all, yelling insanely
for sanity in the murky night, all his rage
turned out. You ask what I remember

of then, the moments that blur
into one length we call *history*
from a distance. What's clear to me: a man
putting his head out the door, on the block,
calling the cops the motherfuckers
they were, without being asked, without
having to. Not letting those blue arms
come down unimpeded was someone I loved.

TRIPS TO THE CLEANER'S

If I had paid already and gone, back
over the pocked and grime-imprinted ice,
I wouldn't have seen the owner come
in fresh-pressed clothes, come on a Sunday,
leaving the children behind. I wouldn't
have heard the rush of his greeting
or seen the young clerk smile
as if an apple sweeter for being stolen
were fresh in her mouth. Her age,
I spent most of most days in my boss' car:
some errand, some pretext to leave the stern
oak desks and printing-ink smell. We'd drive
to the drive-in cleaner, though his wife
had volunteered; we'd pick up the copper plates
for ads — everything in reverse —
though ads weren't his job.

He smoked some sweet mix in a pipe, even then
old-fashioned: arresting and evanescent
as the talk that filled the car. I was enough
of a child to believe everything equally,
enough of a girl to take in his hands, shifting
and steering. Not that we touched — what I knew
of love was Lady Brett and Jake Barnes
with some barrier between them, and
Catherine and Frederick on the run.
When I lay late, listening to my friends wonder
what exactly Scarlett did with Rhett Butler,
I thought I imagined the wedge in my heart.

But his wife grew sharp, her words edged
as if I were important. She took the errands,
I stayed at the desk, calling bereaved families
about funeral plans, editing the Rotary news.
August got clearer, the fields lay shorn,

open to the sun that left them early
and earlier, dark drawing its blade.

I left for the great world he spoke of —
college, and all my life ahead as he promised
so nostalgically, his own life half behind.
I had little past to value, and paid it
little mind. But I paid in my own time,
familiar with strange stories, sudden trips
to the cleaner's. Could I have looked back
when I needed to, I'd have seen the Chevy's
sporty red-and-white, the second run in one day
through the tunnel to pick up the clothes, the man
talking on and I giving the comfort of attention.
Memory might have stretched and embraced
them all: even my husband and the woman drawn
to his hands, his eyes. The man I worked for,
black hair sprang like sea grass from his hands,
his eyes held dangerous water, and I floated
there, oblivious and without hesitation.

DAYS AS GRAY AND BROWN

All the months I drove this road,
lungs full to song — doubtless
there were days as gray and brown —
snow drained away, land adrift
in its losses. I was always slowing
in wonder, then — birds dark stars
over the windshield, and once, October trees
showered their gold, halting both lanes of cars.

The world existed then to be held up
to you, it was marked with your thumb,
hundreds, a thousand miles away. When you came,
it wasn't for me, but something other. Your mouth
took mine late and careless, not knowing how else
to move. I stepped back to see —
nothing for me there but black water.
I slipped, almost pulled all the way down.

Now fields grow rainpools and stubble;
nothing happens to the trees. The brooks
run angry: whitetail spume flying, fleeing —
but the man in the wheelchair bends with sticks
and twine, staking raspberry canes gone rose again.
A spreader lobs manure high, live, over the field,
and farther on, the ground is marked with figure-eights
and circles — some kid on a tractor delirious,
in love as I was all those days with you,
or practicing, pushing the old Harvester
to its limit, the first time purely on his own.

II

TOP OF THE WORLD

There's almost an abundance
of apples — spread in a wide rush
basket, gathered nearby and offered up
so everyone who comes here might eat
and feel at home. Today she's left the kitchen door
open to the bright, still-sharp air that shakes
the kettlesteam in new directions and brings us
in, eager for her talk, her attention, the orders
to set the tea things out, slice the cake,
as in a family, as she rinses the sturdy pot
until steam rises in the shape of its china belly.

She's "older," as we say, meaning at almost
the top of her years, but she wheels the tea-cart
more deftly than we do, quick and young
as the air. She's found a photograph
sixty years old: she and her husband link arms
with an older friend, smiling so directly,
so fearlessly, so open that radiance
transforms the black and white. She says,
"We were on top of the world then,"
with no emphasis on *then*, only pleasure
that makes her face now that face,
though age has made its usual additions
and excisions. On top of the world — it was
Berlin, 1930 — the moment has its moment
again, regardless of how it turned under.

If I have wondered what beauty is,
or why a woman is loved famously, for life,
I see her sudden intake of breath: the joy
undiminished. And the apples that are always
here, or some unfancy fruit of season, are part
of my answer. The basket is shallow, I've said
it's wide, as if made to be held outstretched
while someone climbed a tree. Guided

by advice like hers, but mostly her confidence,
her companion would have climbed free and
fearless, shaken the branches hard without falling,
until the ripe fruit came down.

THE THIRD OF MAY
— AFTER GOYA

Warm against cold, summer
collides with spring. Ache
of white, then flicker, flicker
as if the sky's caught fire.
The wind's on a tear,
bending what bends,
breaking the stubborn trees.

I'm a door loose on its hinge —
but you are calmer than anything
alive. It must have been
those other storms with no forecast
or simple end that taught you:
Head down, keep going, making your sisters laugh,
grateful for your awkward jokes
in the sudden quiet of the neighbors'.

Dark raises its hatchet,
breaks in, but you keep reading
from my book on Goya,
holding the flashlight steady
on the man condemned. You call me
to the cave of his mouth, his arms
outflung, it must be in despair,
as the boots and rifles uniformly poise
to punish on the third of May.

Thunder sends its fusillades
down the sky, rolling close —
but you explain, the white shirt on the page
giving light to your face, how fiercely
the Spanish resisted Napoleon, calling him
great cabbagehead as he cut them down.
It's clear the *guerillero* must be shouting
his last insults, his full-sleeved shirt a snowfield

we know will fill with blood, the white
expanse Goya chose to show —
though surely it was sweat-stained, not new —
as heaviest linen: so much
finer for what lines up against it.

WAKE

Catherine had been dead an hour —
her house and her neighbor's open-mouthed
with light — when we rushed though town
unknowing, so lit by each other we laughed
past the graveyard where your father lay
under a blanket of frost — for him,
no more fast cars rolling everyone to parties,
no more new women and old wounds.

We laughed over old loves — each reminder
of being alive — past the square brick P.O.,
solid and civic, where once my foot slipped
from its shoe and patted the dust, cool,
while the man I'd marry was only beginning
to charm and mislead me. Past the bright porches:
nothing seemed serious that night.
If all the lights meant parties,
we didn't care we weren't asked.

Catherine had been dead just over
an hour when I mentioned the loop
of pearls that always scalloped her neckline,
over the healthy rise of breasts.
She made us feel we might be missing
something, not being old — glossy
in her city black, the furs we'd scorn
on anyone else. "Don't mourn me,"
she'd say, and we didn't know how well
we obeyed her, celebrating, holding
what we didn't know was her wake.

She went on in our talk
as the clock turned toward tomorrow,
as we recalled how couples
we were part of quarreled,

how driving through snow,
they kissed so much they lurched
off the road, and stayed there
a good while, oblivious of cold.

MILKHOUSE

Squat, concrete, made to work —
I never noticed it much — mud and manure
halfway up its sides. This evening, though,
its bare bulbs shone distinct
in the end open to the road: small fists
against the gray that took the fields.
I was driving divided, between places
I love, loose, the car old but imposing,
a rumbler. A boy almost a man
stood in the barn door, hands loosely
linked over a metal bar above him,
sleeves rolled to elbows, elbows
loosely bent. Resting there,
he could read the road: only a few cars
going anywhere, mine clearly on its way
to someplace bright,
rich in chrome, the sweet life glinting from its fenders.

Or so he may have thought, a boy
up every day at four, never free
of cowdung on his shoes, knowing
those smirks in the schoolroom
aim at him. The cows chained in their stanchions
sway slightly to the milk-pump's drone.
The gutters he mucked yesterday need
to be mucked again; his father will yell.
But he faces a little longer away,
he stretches his frame. If every life
were purely sweet — maplesmoke
and leaf mold on the evening air —
he could stay as long as he wants to,
wrists hanging easily from the door-pole,
not secured there: secure.

AIR SHOW

Five bucks a ride, you're part of the sky,
master of distances, light but snug
in the cabin's hold. Five bucks —
the lines are long, but ragged, at ease.
Kids beg for more, men dare one another, bet
on a crash, as the little planes bank and bounce
in, rise and turn again over the gravestones
that nudge the runway, over the plain frames
of houses growing smaller, over the ribbons
of road, the quilt pieced of turning trees.
Upstate, backcorner — the only good job's
guard at the jail; most people never have flown.

Five bucks, chance of your life — my friend
pulls his leather helmet on, steps on the footrest,
then the fighter's shiny wing. Everything stills —
even the pennants on the kids' bigwheels, the burgers
hissing on the grill. I feel the looks: curious,
fearful, in sympathy. We all know
there's no time to glide —
a plane so fast and heavy will fall hard
if the engine goes. We may be watching something
eternal: the moment that etches in memory
as the last of a thing.

My friend
holds the windshield and slides down in.
Thumbs up — Herb holds an extinguisher
ready. Thumbs up — burst of exhaust, rush
of several tons past gravity, and we're taken
in the rise, the dive, the vanishing,
breathless, as someone who loves flight
or is brave or gives little value to his life
cuts the sky in half.
        We can't see or hear now,
we press our faces up to the emptiness, the wondering

why —
The returning roar, the bold arc
and swoop and slice above the crowd
push the heart past hesitation. Brian points —
a hawk not far off is doing it differently,
just lazing on the air. What we want:
to be that effortless, that light, believing
machines can change us. But there is still
only the one life, and my friend chooses to take it
on the wing, with no glidetime. We clap and cheer,
released, as he slides in, alive to his chances.

FALL

It was worse for you,
hearing the stumble of tangled feet,
cry of panic
more than pain, feeling — you said —
your balls shrink inside
when you saw how I'd met concrete:
cheek, lip, elbow crashed
on the hard, the real.

I'd been lost
in your face, the sky arched
over us, the fields open
as that day I'd seized for my work,
with you nearby. I forgot
the details that ground
any enterprise, and the ground rose,
insulted, and took my feet in its grip.

You cursed yourself for not finishing
that terrace, the rough place
that trapped me in pain at the simplest
turn of the wrist, in a cast awkward
as Frankenstein, trying to assure you
there's triumph that the cork rises
in the corkscrew, the wine enters
the glass, the door knob is coaxed to yield.

The moon through icicles makes
a new galaxy — close to us, delirious.
Though time is measured in small moves,
the long *after* reflects the *before*
that made it — the snowless morning;
my book open to Chekhov landing
on the island that changed his life;
you having nothing else on hand
for healing, using your lips
as the balm for my scraped and swollen face.

DOG STAR

I didn't know what star it was:
riding west, fist in the window, too bright
where all light should dim for the dog
who shivered, and from so deep in
I had to bend to hear, gave a thin,
continuing call. Longer than I lived
with my parents, longer than marriage,
than my child stayed home, longer
than any other love, she lasted: heart
of the house, singer of undoglike cadenzas,
bucking in the stiff gait
of the last years, meeting each day's breath
with ears on alert and tail beating allegro,
out flirting when dogs her age are flat
by the fire. The only being with no flaw —

unless I count her greedy stretch
to nip someone else's food. By the end,
all mischief was gone, her nose cracked
like old leather, eyes full of cloud
and every bone articulate. When I touched her
those last times, I felt the tremor —
the body's voice saying: Now I falter,
now I go on; now I am sinking — but there's
a flash of taste, sunlight there — and now
I can take no more of this world.

Was it the Dog Star that woke me
with its shine? Hours before dawn
I found the dog shaking in the warm house,
heard as I lay against her, the low note,
all she'd allow herself of plea. Stumbling
on us in the dark, Mitch laid his blunt hand
lightly on my head, shy of this closer relation.
I said I'd give anything
to have the dog young; he thought I meant

having the whole past back.
I wanted her as she was: quick, alive.

The star that watched till dawn
must have been Sirius, the dog one,
faithfully circling its master, in the bond
that just *is*, that we call dumb or blind,
as if it's senseless to just keep on,
to love some things without question.

IMAGINARY TWIN

He was the one hid with me,
run from the seekers, to the closet
to hold our breath — *one* breath —
among the rags and brooms, the mop's
unkempt hair, bucket's torturous vise,
soap powder and ammonia unbearably
scratching our noses.

I could say *our* so easily then,
he was that close to me, the one
I made, had named — *Perry*,
because that sounded daring:
smart and tough. "This is Perry,"
proudly I'd introduce him
to my parents, to visible friends.
I'd sense him there.

He wasn't the usual substitute
for all I'd done wrong — I was too
attached. No one tried —
in this I was blessed — to take him
from me, or point out what was *really*
real. Where was the child, after all,
who might have been there:
the one who was willed away?

Imagination filled the still house
with brothers and sisters, the trees
on the placid lawn with families —
a town — of friends. It was a harmless
happiness, my parents could see,
but absence must have opened in them
whenever I said, "my brother."

Perry has a sharp, a piercing
sound. I didn't know — or did I? —
I used it like a knife. The baby
who came later was truly my kin,
but he seemed then so small to me,
more child than my brother.

Someone my size was already beside me;
he was all my need. When then
did the twin leave me, when did I
begin to look for someone so attuned?
Must I keep wanting that you abide
as silently, steadily with me —
not asking anything, not disputing:
not being you?

CHEEK TO CHEEK

It was really more stomach
to stomach: the chicken wire
stiff blue of my best dress
mashed to the cummerbund
of Elly's older brother, who smelled
of whisky and murky aftershave.
I didn't have much to interest
him, but those sixteen-year-old sharks
in satin lapels knew how to press
the girls' bodies the full length
of theirs. Whatever there was,
they'd feel — except for the tidal
drift below the waist, guarded
by crinoline and net. Except for the way
we shook, proud and old with change,
when the music ended and we were released.

All the bright, wise songs that could send
Fred Astaire across a ceiling — but we
barely moved our feet, finding in the beat
only what was soggy and slow. I remember
lodging my chin on a collar bone, relieved
of the need to speak. Oh, the wit and the perfectly
matched height of the movie dancers, cheek
touching cheek meaning two moving as one,
never knocking knees or having to think
which corner of the imaginary box
to step to next. I think my life was saved
by rock and roll — you could do anything,
dance was how you wanted it — far apart
or close to, some guy who stole cars
through college kissing your hand
on the back-again of a flying turn.
Nothing to hold onto, just motion
over hardwood and linoleum floors.

And then I'm not young, but dancing
as if the old song is new to the air,
dancing out the flight I want, the stamp
that drives the memory of dancesteps
into the ground, the shake of the head
that tosses off bad times. The stir that
begins again, dancing my heart out — not *away,*
but up from the inside, to where it shows.
I don't touch my partner, don't have to,
need no insurance — we're so attuned —
to glide just tonight up the wall, across
the ceiling, smooth, and no question, cheek to cheek.

"I CAN'T GET STARTED," THAT SLOW

Between the exhaled breath
the note rides on and the audible intake
when the player takes his lips
from his horn, the music
hears itself, the after-sound
vibrating with what's gone,
the next note suspending
in the pause: the other shoe
that takes its own sweet time to fall.

Each break in the tune
makes the listeners know
listening, and if it's
Lucky Thompson on tenor sax
and the song's "I Can't Get Started,"
he *is* in luck, whatever else
he's had or lost, being *in*
this life, slowing the bright
line of notes to make
another time, or home.

With nothing to play on
but time, you stayed
when I thought you'd be gone,
walked me to work, so slow
I thought a stone caught in your shoe.
You leaned back as I
pressed on; when you spoke,
the words didn't want to be
strung together. Each waited
for a different tune, not the one
written beforehand: no question
of getting started, every answer
wanting to. In the space
between word and word, step
and step, wasn't that the life
we wouldn't have together?

You took my bag of books, bold
and shy as a schoolkid, swung
its weight from your shoulder,
noticed a leaf lodged in my hair.
With your touch I was still,
almost at my office door, the end
of our tune, the pause
that stretches out after,
going deaf from hearing itself
so well: hiss of blank tape,
no new notes but your fingers slow
to separate the strands of my hair
so the green aspen-leaf heart
could come free without hurting.

FATHER AND SON

Late light spreads, calm, and we
have to be in awe of it, lost
in it, losing the threads of want
and grievance, defiance and desire
that wind through all the stories
we offer one another. He loves
this time of day purely, with no reservation,
and the moment stretches its bowstring out
until the boy snaps it, home
in the mesh football shirt with his number,
his face clear: white quartz
without a chip, just some abrasion
at the edges, asking without asking
Who is this woman who seems so at home
with his father? The light gets lighter,
loses substance, ready to leave.

The fires must be fed, hay thrown
to the sheep; the boy will do one,
the man the other, keeping the farm
a while alive. The man takes his coat
for the muddy yard, his eyes moving
with an Arctic ocean's glitter
and dangerous tide. His lips taste
of cider's hard edge and sweet
fallen fruit that I drink and thirst for
until I lose my balance, shocked
then against the fence of his bones.

The boy is taking potatoes he's helped
harvest from their burlap nest,
cradling them in one wide hand
before he slices the geode-crust
to white quartz. Small moons slide
into the black sky on the burner;
garlic teeth slip from cover,

and some salt stars. Slower than his father,
calm, he cracks the eggs as deftly —
four suns land brilliantly whole
in the galaxy of moons. I'm praying
that his eyes stay so open, his sight
so clear, making homefries and eggs
so carefully for a father lifting bales
unsteadily, cursing the sheep,
trusting only that fire is dissolving
the wood he split, giving substance
to the eggs he culled, softening potatoes
for the moment's pleasure they'll give
his tongue. Trusting most the cider's amber
that preserves bruised fruit and losses.

ADDICTION

Young, I didn't understand: each breath
was a mouthful of dust — and the doctor, perfect
gentleman, angel of deliverance, held the flesh
of her damp, intimate inner arm between thumb
and first finger as if weighing silk.
He showed her how easily the needle
could slide home. On fire but not burning:
dancing, leaving the pale body a shadow
on the bed, looking down from the ceiling
at the sentries bearing oxygen, at the sprays,
the powders and capsuled consolations.

People wondered was he her lover,
shut in, secret, so often and long.
Silver hair, correct in a high starched collar
years after changes in style, cold sky
in his pupils — he never gave himself
to any woman but took everyone's secret —
not just the bared flesh he saw coolly,
to treat it, but the cry at the knife's edge,
the plea for deliverance. She shook
before him, and he showed her how
to pinch the loose flesh herself,
gave her the recipe for almost-oblivion.

Opening to the night, she could breathe then,
take in air enough to fly, spreading her arms
to the buoyant possibility. All the voices rising
from the narrow pews told me
Flesh is nothing, Life is a fever
to get over. She seemed to agree,
using music and words, the long skeins
of her knitting to sustain her.
I didn't know I could burn so —
but today a look, a voice
take over my veins again, running so free
and fast I'm rudderless and shaken.

When her survivors found the formula
she'd so carefully written, and hidden,
in the Shakespeare no one else would read,
she was past the flesh-fever and the shame
that made them close the book
and burn the page. If I had known then,
if I'd lived in a family that didn't believe
in protecting its own, I'd have been still
and unbending as the stained glass angel
filtering light through the church. But the secret
slips unbidden, out of its time into the right time,
when I see her flesh as mine — long neck,
narrow feet, eyes for men — and all the other
parts that ask just to be seen for themselves:
wanting — how it is with humans.

WORLD'S END

Pale sky through a square high
on a bare wall — I saw my death
there: no one near, no beauty or oddness
to distract me. No help, none for it, no
getting free — I caught a glimpse of it
this morning, but turned and moved
into the day that waited cold in all the rooms
for my motion to fill it. I think you'd
recognize how absence finds a palpable shape, and why
when I came into town this middle of morning
and saw no one, no car or soul moving there
or in the next town, no gust even
of exhaust, it seemed the world
had ended, everyone had fled
some danger I was ignorant of, alone.
Oh, God — but there was none.
I went on, and other cars
began their ordinary conversations.

You'd have known, had I told you then,
but the woman you'd brought to the party
talked of *World's End* as a street of London,
and some shred of tact kept me from showing
you were seeing the end of all things. I didn't tell
anyone, most of all you, how outside the house the moon
sailed pure and full-sailed as the one the old painter set
floating on turquoise enamel, casting its eye, benevolent,
on the couple holding hands. They're in costume, on the way
to a ball, or from, I think, escaping delirious
into the maze and shelter of woods. I could have
called your attention, I knew you listened
though I didn't look, and no matter what I said.
Silent, I could float a little longer in no
hurry or relation, before a new world shapes itself
in our image and we find its limits. Let them this time
be unusual: not between us, but infinite, around.

FERRY PERMIT

Nebraska — it's brassy, grassy, broad
in my mind; I forget which rectangle
you said it was in the middle of the map.
The snow- or rain-lines seem everywhere anyway
in the big belly-section every time I look.
You have to fly through just one part,
but on a ferry permit, not knowing the plane,
any space is vast.
When I think of you in the snow sky,
idly, with no fear of loss, it's like
no love, or a marriage too old for questions.

You land in my kitchen all angles,
sensing yourself too large, too loud,
in the space I wanted untroubled, mine.
You're stunned from it — forced down,
one engine out, the ceiling low, trees
straight ahead, and the plane's nose
heavy, reluctant. Gravity reached,
and almost had you, but you
make it light: "Old plane, ferry permit,
what else can you expect?"

Charon
knew his barge — black, sleek, high
on the sides to keep the disembodied
souls from slipping — and of course knew
how to pole through Styx's swift water.
If he thought you'd be aboard, you surprised
him: too bright for that
still and gloomy place.

But the boy
whose toy the plane was to be — scarcely old
enough to fly or kill himself, killed himself
as you ferried home his plane. I forget
what I meant to say — wanting that evening
alone, being drawn to someone else.
Fact blanks out thought; you almost died,
as the boy did, for no reason. Fact, like the ground
that rose to claim you — too large, too hard,
too dark. It leaves no room for fine points.
I look at you, wanting no other thing.

BODY OF EARTH

The hills speak to us up here,
through the wind off their peaks
and up from their hollows, shaking,
bumping the small plane.
We trace the scars of winter
on their broad backs; some trees,
you say, won't green this year.
The frozen swamp turns to us
its blind face, hiding nothing
from our inspection: beaver hump, stubble
of trunks, lines where snow machines whined over.

The arcing sky fills the cabin, affable,
so generous with light it takes
my silent cry: *We are so small, the plane*
old; there's my house empty, and so much
yet to be done... Your hands know
the wheel, your eyes the dangers
of high terrain. We look it over
together — Town Hall seeming so sure
in its greening square; bare ground
and brash new timber where once were
fields and woods, those trees you wandered in,
up from the river that soothed you as a child.

We go low, learning the familiar body
in new ways: suddenly naked, suddenly almost
ours. Face to face with us, it lies
so open, breathes so deep, stretches
and turns in its long sleep, asking
so little it's easy to think it feels
nothing, giving and not reckoning
the gift. Taking every wound dumbly.
We come down, dazed from being
so intimate, this other body vast
inside us, alive — meaning able to die.

III

BLADE

The sun as it sets lights the beech wood
red through all the arches and alleyways
of branches — more complex than any
cathedral, but like one: dusty grays,
brilliant illuminations. And across fields,
the furrows stand up in sharp relief — not bare,
shorn of dry corn and scattered with the teeth
of stalks the cutting left behind.
In the hard clarity November brings
you can see the old land's secrets: delicate
weeds, the comfort of hollows, rocks
in archaic formations. But to the boy
pulling the rip-cord, holding the chainsaw hard
against the jump of the first cut into wood,
this place has an emptiness always the same —
dumb trees, blank sky, flat field. The saw
forces the wood to answer, to fall.

The door gives on an empty house, space
holds still as he enters: it's his.
And he takes in his power some shiny thing
he knows is good to trade — for warmth,
for ease, to forget the bare table
in flat blue light, assaults
of silence, curses almost relief.
Child not a child, the muscles tightening,
lengthening, the beard's mark
fallen on your face, can you see what I have the luck to?
This moon a fat cat in the milk, mountains
losing their heads to mist — no matter
what I lose, I'll always find this.

Over you, turning your music
hard against silence, scattering
field mice in the spin of your tires,
the moon hangs, lowering its blade.

WINDFALLS IN SNOW

These falls I've let the apples go,
falling into no baskets but the grasses',
breaking apart for Indian Summer wasps,
shrinking and freezing to blood-drops
on the branches, waiting bruised for deer
who every night write their stories in the snow
of the orchard. Up late, later,
I watch for them in vain. No dark
cover enough, no hour quite still.

Now, though, under curtains of snow,
in day as broad as such a dim one gets,
a young doe steps from the screen
of trees, from her unseen life. Legs thin
as the youngest trunks, she roots for apples
in the snow. The soft scene — snow blurring
already shaggy pines, blurring fur —
seems almost made to be seen: a rare preserve.

But to come so far, to stay
so exposed — she must be starved.
A dog cracks the quiet, but the doe still
lowers her head, deaf to everything
but the teeth in her gut, the new life
that distends her. I could leave her
our leavings — grapefruit's half-suns,
celery's white heels — but dogs too would be drawn:
the whole neighborhood of them gleeful, overtaking her in snow.

What is it draws me
from shelter? As if nothing ends,
nothing is let go, you call
after years, teasing as always, cajoling:
Will I drive the snowy road to meet you?
The same voice, knowing and low,
led me through all obstacles, made light

of weather. In precarious places
we'd laugh and argue and look
for wordless answers in each other.

Now, though, the light stays dim and even.
Snow keeps thickening the hill,
and I make it my reason, letting day
close without moving. The deer stay still,
intent. Have I grown old, and un-
adventurous? Or is there something else
to love: snowfall and the deer under it,
nose tunnelling after windfalls.

BIG WHITE ONE, EWIE,
LITTLE BLACK NOSE

At five weeks, and always before I'm ready,
the big white one brays for his milk,
lunges against the makeshift fence,
teaching the others to follow.
Part of their strength comes from the jostling
they do, displacing one another,
pawing the scrap-wood and any curly back in their way,
as they strain for more time at the nipple.
The two left out suck all extremities
with their daily sharper teeth. They pull the bottle so, if I don't
    hold hard
it flies, is gone, leaking, under their hooves.
All their wish for life — their hunger — telegraphs
from their throats through their springing jaws
to the nerves of my arm.

Before they could stretch
to the top of the fence, I went in
to them, kneeling on straw, lifting and holding each,
trying to replace the mother who failed them —
one with no milk to give, the other
who ignored her young. The ewe
whose twins strangled inside her
would accept no substitutes, calling the first day
and through the night for the ones she lost.
Such a human thing, or is grief
more *animal*? She couldn't get over it,
and went with the others roughly penned
on the flatbed to spend their last night
crowded together there, going to auction
in the morning, silent at the strangeness
of being five feet off the ground,
who can say not stunned from being so far
from their familiar field? They turned

their Assyrian profiles away from me,
against the sunset, then the dark.
When all lambs must end like that,
why should I feel so much is gone?

In new fields now with the flock,
the ones I sheltered must shiver
in this rain through their fleece.
Who now will dry them, keep them
from harm? The time I don't spend on them
still isn't free; I held them too much,
looked too long at the knowing slant
of their wide-set eyes. Big White One, Ewie,
Little Black Nose — I couldn't help
giving them names. Would I care so for sheep
if it weren't for Anne, grown, so far beyond my shelter?

TOWARD GUATEMALA

1.

It was so easy to be a tourist.... It was only
with time that you could see. (Jennifer)

In the place between sleep and sleep,
sparrows grew teeth, a body with no arms
or legs threw itself toward a bowl
on a prison floor. A woman in deep green
clung to a rail as the ceiling pressed her
down. A jester — white gloves, black cape,
whiteface and mascara — aimed a gun
so slowly I thought I could stop him,
but you turned towards his fire
and were struck above the eye.

You didn't tell me your dreams,
but something forced you from sleep
screaming, upright and held
in a place darker than your midnight room.
When you cry out there, half-rise,
will someone real be splitting the door?

The skull is beautiful; it stands for the plain truth.

2.

The first night I could sleep without waking
in fear that they would come to arrest me was
my first night out of my country.
        —Rigoberta Menchu

Your friends took the danger
lightly, having lived through it
themselves — one with scars
on her arm — telling stories of death threat

though you were hiding him and his father,
candles on the cake the only light,
shutters fast against the heat.

Give us a steady light, a level place,
  a good light, a good place,
  a good life and beginning.

8.
I can't tell you why, but my fear disappeared
... [I]t had become so clear to me, how much
                it was worth.
              (Bernardo)

River through a narrow channel, the crowd
moves off the plane — no one I know, no one,
then hair like yours, something black, strong-colored,
boots, pack, wave. You blur in the same myopic joy
that came when you slid from my body. *I love it*
there, you say, and later, not unkind, *You have*
to let go, as in the dream you shook me off,
insisting you were fine: no blood, just an inkblot
on your temple. The body I saw falling short,
falling short, falling face-first into watery beans
was mine, not yours. The figure holding the rope
in the river, wasn't that me, being pulled under?
And aren't you and your companions the ones who wade in,
though the current runs cold and could take you —
sparrows startling and settling —
and bring me to stand on shore.

How should it be sown? How should it dawn? ... They are not dead.
They have merely made a way for the light to show itself.

End-Note:

The first quotation in every section is from Jennifer Harbury's
   Bridge of Courage, an oral history of the Guatemalan resistance
   movement. The second quotation in every section is from the
   Popul Vuh as translated by Dennis Tedlock.

THE CHILDREN
FROM GIOVANNI DI PAOLO'S "RAISING OF LAZARUS"

Before perspective or shadows or names —
he is only John, son of Paul; before
mistakes could be revised, each stroke
being indelible on the hardening wall;
before doubt, which is the consciousness
of self; before the expression of doubt,
the painter gave to his flat, clear shapes
a solid definition: Lazarus green from the grave,
with the odd sheep-like eyes those Italians
thought eastern; the crowd at the tomb
as one shape — hilly landscape or cloud —
each robed body and mane of hair
lapped against the next.

Some heads have the gold scallop,
that coin the holy wear; those are the ones
who stare awed and almost smiling at the gaping
tomb. But others, no halos,
cover their noses; one even gags from the stench
Lazarus brings: vomit spraying delicately down
on dotted lines from a red-lipped oval
rimmed by chicklet teeth. All of them frown.

Christ stands of course at the center,
larger, welcoming Lazarus back to the world —
the dark desert with its mountains
that loom darker, more forbidding still.
It will take faith and courage to step
from the cave of the tomb towards the watchers,
into this landscape where little lives. Christ
will be the magnet, but what drew me most
wasn't that expected beard and blessing
hand. The painter has added something
on his own — two children,
heads too large for their bodies. Us,
the plaque explains — the watching world.

Back to back, almost joined —
one looks at the disciples and Christ,
the other at Lazarus half-decayed.
One side all spirit and overcoming,
the other by what the body comes to
overcome. The heads, the heads
are what stopped me at this picture.
They look up open-mouthed, the way
all children do. You know, when they stumble
from sleep onto a scene they can make no sense of,
that paints itself as fresco does: instant,
indelible in the soft, blank wall.

FULL FLOWER MOON

The moon develops the earth, and prints it
platinum, the sky's grey a bit bluer,
barely distinct against the stars.
Full Flower they called this moon
when people noticed degrees
of bloom, when there was little but blooming
to notice, and all the blossoms
opened in their proper time.
High over the fields, the radio signal
winks its red eye, competing, knowing
where the Northway stretches its coils.

The valley stretches out from here
as if it would never close, the land
still breathing through mouths of clover
and vetch. Beauty is this openness:
your hand that won't turn against me,
the width of your untroubled cheek,
the pollen of lashes fanning across.

We drive out the old hay-track, buoyed
by alfalfa and light, the scent of thyme
released by crushing, the lollop of hills
running parallel, each moving by eons
into its own shape. So surrounded,
we try to say what beauty is, or makes —
our standing awed together here, inundated
by space and shadowless light. And how
when something stretches so open and limitless,
someone who feels himself made small
in comparison will itch to enter,
place his mark on a body so trusting, so
unsuspecting he thinks it will be easy
to make it his own size, as the red eye
gives him its blessing, more constant
than the moon, but bringing nothing to flower.

BREAK OF DAY: AFTER COLETTE

Wherever I move: the scent of mint,
overgrowing the garden, choking off
cilantro, tarragon, dill and now
beginning to brown at its edges.
I've never had the heart for uprooting,
or even chopping tentacles
where they've branched and dig in.
And the stalks are so high
they screen me from the road
where I soak in the last sun that warms
the granite step, though the chill
from shadowed ground seeps into it.

In my book, there are herbs in abundance:
flowering, spilling over rock walls.
The woman thins and transplants,
pinches basil for her soup, and looks up
unstartled as the young man, Vial,
swings on her garden gate. She doesn't think
he comes into her kitchen like sunlight;
the sun itself has found the peppers
in her cobalt bowl, lemons tumbled across tile.
                    She'll tell him
by the book's end — I'm re-reading,
so I know — to marry the young woman
who wants him, with whom he can have
marriage, a child. To love is to want
the other's best, isn't it so?
Her dignity is perfect, unshakable.
For herself — *Who said you should be happy?*
Do your work — the clarity of solitude.

            Vial will make a feeble
counter-argument, and soon be on his way
to young love without regret, with only
affection for the older woman who sheltered and taught.

No one has said anything regrettable,
indelible, no dishes been thrown,
tears burned into cheeks — which is why
I'm reading Colette again, except
that the young love of her late years
loved and never left her; she was only
imagining him gone. If she had seen
my Vial, could she have thought of weeding
her life of him so calmly and surely,
as I should now be dragging the mint's runners
out of the damp ground? If she had seen
the one I thought would be my Vial
once I had seen him.

YELLOW GLADIOLAS
(IN MEMORY OF WILLARD SQUIER)

He must have seen me coming,
my need that day spilling all over the road.
He took from the cans of gladiolas
one bunch, yellow, and held it out
to me — a gallantry entirely unlike him —
This is for you.

Old ones,
I thought, somehow spoiled for sale —
In all the years I'd come to him
for the freshest corn, not bothering now
to strip down a ribbon of green to see,
the kernels always sweet, firm, exactly pearls,
he'd hardly given me a nod,
his face too hardened by years of sun
and losing things — land, wife, health:
the riches of his youth — to bend much
toward a smile. He couldn't have known
what it meant — that day when hope
had left me. Couldn't have known,
as when my grandmother — not knowing
the only flowers for sale were gladiolas
in the French village that Saint's Day,
so my young parents had to buy a bunch,
something to lay on the soldier's grave
they'd come so far to find among so many —
not knowing, sent my mother as she'd never done
or did again, bulbs that fall,
that came up tall-stalked, furled blossoms:
formal, funereal, Gladiolus.
                            But these yellows
the farmer lays in my car are a cloud
of butterflies — the kind called puddle —

an innocence of yellow, an abundance
that lasts and lasts, longer
than I expected: a flutter, a drop
in the dry well of the heart.

RURAL DELIVERY

She's come a hard way,
down the steep drive, two kids
on the sled and one running,
the dog heedless, heading
cross-lots ahead.

Come
for the mail, the flat pillows
cold from the truck and metal box,
scented with seductive exhaust.

        Stock-still
in the road, she shifts the pale pallets
along her arm — nothing here
but numbers pointing sharp angles
at the heart, dead words
addressed to no one alive.

She sifts again, unable to identify
what she looks for, or why
her heart banged its empty boxcar
through fields.

        Along the road,
someone older and slow
makes her way to the metal loaf — what food is there?

        If only one soul
will recognize another, greeting those red metal arms
that are waiting and waving —

        If only the way were smooth
        If only more
will be legible in the landscape
           than what I see:
        Quill marks
corn stubble makes at random on the field's white page.

WITHIN THE DOOR: DICKINSON'S ROOM
(DARE YOU SEE A SOUL *AT THE WHITE HEAT* THEN CROUCH WITHIN THE DOOR —)

Crowded in, as many as fit
with a guide, who of us
can find a soul here?
A room chaste, light,
well-made. Grate empty
of ash, narrow bed for one
unnarrow soul, writing table
too slight, it seems, to stand
the jolt and jab of that pen.
Branches in each window, glimpses
to feed the soul sky. Scarlet
blanket for a gardener's white
organdy knees, paisley bloodstream
staining the virginal quilt —
I see and still am so far
from how she saw — though this door
must have been *the* door,
and where I am *within*,
incomplete as I am: so many paths
and days of inconsequence, words
slipping away, the soul unmet.

Her fifty-five years seemed
a long life, until I had as few.
Will I make nothing new, nothing
of value? Her room gives
no answer; in solitude her words
come: *Dare you.* What if no one
speaks back? It's not like her
to leave home or urge a stranger,
but this voice is hers: harsher,

blunter than I've imagined: *Crouch* —
What else can I do? If the rest
of this life is to be anywhere
near nearly enough —

FOOD FOR THE DEAD
— FOR KITTY HAMILTON

Because they feared the footsteps,
the shadow tugging at the edge of sight,
they laid out bread for them,
a film of soup on the bottom of the bowl,
a spoon. From hard, unremarked lives
to hard, unremembered deaths —
bread to quiet them in their restless
resting places — But how could they rest
with so much left undone?

> *Age 37, wife of*
> *and mother. Cut down*
> *before the canning could be finished —*

> *Gone to God —*

no, still lingering over the living,
unable to go. Are the floors swept,
does the lilac still bloom?
To soothe them, then, the table
set at night when the house is silent.

But Kitty, I'm calling you back
to be with us — not just with me,
because even in life I faltered
at the flood of your emotion, laughed
at your torment, once, not to feel it.
I mean, keep speaking: make us keep seeing
the wedge of the vole's step in snow;
beauty in the bones of your brother's fingers
ringing the trigger of the gun filling his mouth.

When I called to give your poems praise
I understood that knot of a sob
in your throat. You understood this

was your life's sentence: to declare
what you saw, to help us see until you
could no longer make the sounds,
the cancer killing them — and refused
al! compromise, meaning more life.

Are you anywhere near?
I'm putting out not bread
but blank paper. Do you like
this kind of pen, staying up late,
your hand guiding mine?

HEALING
(IN MEMORY OF PEPPER CONSTABLE)

If the tests come out wrong, if the cells
begin to fail in their quiet weaving;
if the body that so lightly carries
this life betrays me — some night
when the pines talk to one another,
when no moon would tell my secret, snow
would fill my steps, I could go to that hill
so far beyond my neighbor's it has no name.
Walking and waiting for numbness, I'd feel
the blade of air I'd chosen for my chest.
And if winter were too far away, the water
I watched today could take me — swift
churn of Otter Creek Falls, fanning out
smooth, moving from shore. Entering
such depth, a body would be part
of a motion, alive in its last time.

The doctor sensed the first tear
in his own tissue. The hand
with scythe-neat nails began to belong
to someone rebellious, his feet
were marble boats headed different ways,
his tongue turned against the thoughts
that tried to guide it. His country lost
its history — the childhood house
with its swings and boxwood borders,
the woman he noticed as she turned away.
He dreamed of dusty arenas, every exit
barred, a roar coming from the bull chute.

Doctor, he knew there'd be no reversal;
no way to cut or soothe. The ocean was open
all the way to the skyline: generous and deep.
How did he choose the time — after a day
of stumbling, or one so bright it tempted him

to stay? One night of no moon, he listened
to his wife breathing deep and even,
slipped back the broad cuff of sheet. Standing,
he let his nightclothes fall like snakeskin,
rustling down. He stepped into the last future
he could make — cold salt marking his ankles,
his calves as he waded in. Thighs, balls,
belly, chest. The tide began to love him
then, its pulse pressing his nipples,
answering his heart. He kept on,
letting in the water that would be his new air,
opening to the larger world, the failed body
lost to the final healing.

THE YELLOW TRANSPARENTS

An early apple, a summer one
that doesn't keep, it grows only
in dooryards or orchards
lost to brambles and weeds.

> *You'd shake the tree*
> *to get, say, twenty apples maybe you'd use*
> *right away...*

He climbed and shook the branches,
his little sister cut and peeled,
filling the round, quart-sized bowl.

> *She made them for me.*
> *I was ten, that made her seven.*
> *I wanted to eat them*
> *like a horse, so I put my mouth right here —*

He leans to his table —

> *and began to eat apples and eat*
> *apples. I finally ate every one I could get,*
> *couldn't get every one. I was so full of apples*
> *when I started for the cows ...*

up in the highest pasture, climbing, slowing,
lying down, hoping to still
the churn of his innards,
climbing on, *his* job to bring the cows down.

> If the past
wouldn't go so fast, he could be
so sturdy still — even last year
he scythed his near meadow. He could be
climbing still, his sister peeling
a quart of apples just for him, in the love

of seven years old, the yellow transparents
falling from her knife.

        It must have taken her
a long while, with hands that size, but they had to use
the apples, they wouldn't keep —

I gave you what I could, knowing
it wouldn't last, wasn't nearly enough.
The last summer light over the fields now
brightens just before it goes,
leaving the leaves it's turned gold,
the early apples with their transparent skin.
You can almost see the apple-flesh;
you can see your whole life through it.

THE OTHER ROAD

Soft air, soft light from an apple-slice moon,
clouds bunching and dispersing around it.
Just enough stars to make a crooked path
that runs parallel to the one
where I walk the dog by rushes and halts,
her nose drawn to the thread of brook,
a graze of grass, to something ripely
dead, where she hurls herself down
to make that smell her own.

       Except,
tonight, she doesn't roll from side to side,
but lies still, as if she wants to hold
the night with its scents, its washing light.
Or as if she wants it to hold her,
in perfect permanence.

       As good as it gets,
dear dog — Minute by minute a fan of cloud
opens over the moon, the breeze takes on
the brook's chill, and I ache to keep
the sky before the cloud, *and* the cloud,
and the other road of stars growing less
and less clear, the growing more
clouded, and the boundary, alive
as if someone draws it, between them.

Joan Aleshire grew up outside Baltimore, Maryland, and graduated from Harvard/Radcliffe College. Twenty years later, she entered the MFA Program for Writers at Goddard College, and received her degree in 1980. Her first book of poems, *Cloud Train*, was published in 1982 by Texas Tech Press, and her second book, *This Far*, appeared in 1987. She lives in Vermont and has taught in the MFA Program for Writers at Warren Wilson College since 1983.